TRADITION AND IN

The Pottery of New Mexico's Pueblos

by Linda B. Eaton

Museum of Northern Arizona

Above: Contemporary Zuni vases featuring snake and lizard appliques and contemporary Zuni bowl
with lizard motifs by Priscilla Peynetsa, upper left, 1987; center and lower right, 1990
Opposite page: Contemporary Zuni duck effigy pot by Darrell Westika and Priscilla Peynetsa, 1990

INTRODUCTION

The pottery of New Mexico's Pueblo Indians is among the most varied and beautiful of traditional southwestern arts. Its uniqueness made it a popular collector's item by the late nineteenth century. Anthropologists for large Eastern museums collected it extensively in the 1870s, and travelers and other aficionados of Indian life followed closely upon their heels.

In the twentieth century, another type of buyer, one who saw the pieces as something more than a reminder of the collector's own travels or a visual record of cultures passing away, began acquiring Pueblo pottery. These new buyers saw in the fruits of the potters' labors genuine works of art. Their receptivity opened the door economically to the continuation of pottery as an art form through this century and into the next.

In the collections assembled with this new attitude, including the Museum of Northern Arizona pieces featured here, there are great varieties of beautiful and innovative works in traditions that span many centuries. In addition to their beauty, however, the pots and figurines have many other stories to tell, for the story of Pueblo pottery is also one of trade, conquest, closeness to cities and railroad lines, powerful individual personalities, and shifting inter-village relationships during the past two-thousand years. Crosscurrents of exchange and communication among many peoples are visible in the ceramics.

But more than any of these things, it is a reaffirmation and recreation of Pueblo life, drawn and modeled from the flesh of Mother Earth through the hands of the potter. These individuals often speak of the pots in terms reserved to life forms, and the designs they utilize are important symbols related to the life of the fields, the animals, and the people themselves.

The Pueblo Indians of New Mexico include sixteen different tribes from five distinct language groups, most of whom live along the Rio Grande and its tributaries. An exception is the Pueblo of Zuni, whose inhabitants' language has no known relatives. Their village is located on a tributary of the Little Colorado, and the people are more similar in many ways to the Hopi of Arizona than to the puebloans of the Rio Grande.

The technological categories of historic Pueblo pottery coincide roughly with the language groupings of its makers. Most interaction and organization among the Pueblos, including the actual locations of the villages as well as the diversity of their pottery, directly reflect these language relationships. The Tewa-speaking pueblos of San Ildefonso, Santa Clara, San Juan, Tesuque, Nambe, and Pojoaque are clustered just north of Santa Fe. This area has produced perhaps the most famous of all Pueblo potters—San Ildefonso's Maria Martinez—who gave Tewa pottery its trademark, polished red and blackwares.

The Tiwa-speaking pueblos—Taos and Picuris, Isleta and Sandia—come from two distinct Tiwa-language political groups that existed at the time of the Spanish Entrada. Their pottery clearly reflects these two different histories. Taos and Picuris have virtually indistinguishable glittering micaceous ware; in Isleta and Sandia, traditional pottery making has nearly vanished. The sole remaining Towa-speaking pueblo, Jemez, produces a brown-on-tan ware almost exclusively.

The speakers of Keresan languages, from Zia, Acoma, Santa Ana, Cochiti, San Felipe, Santo Domingo, and Laguna, also produce pottery recognizable as a group, favoring plant and animal forms in black or black and red on a white background. Zuni-speakers' work is as unique as their language—elaborate black-on-white and polychromes in the past and a variety of elaborately painted white, red, and buffwares today.

A BRIEF HISTORY

The Pueblo Indians of New Mexico are the descendants of the prehistoric people we call the Anasazi—with the exception of the Zunis, who probably combine Anasazi origins with the ancestry of another prehistoric culture, the Mogollon. These people lived to the south of what is now Zuni territory. The Mesa Verde, Chaco, and San Juan Anasazi to the north are probably the main groups represented in the ancestry of the current New Mexico pueblos.

The making and use of pottery has been one of the important identifying characteristics of the Pueblos, past and present, from as far back as 300 B.C., when pottery first appeared among the Mogollon. Most authorities believe that the technology spread northward from Mesoamerica, through the Mogollon and their western neighbors (the Hohokam), to the Anasazi in the third century A.D. There is evidence that this early pottery often was formed using a basket as support, a process that left distinct impressions on the soft clay.

Archaeologists use the durable prehistoric ceramics to help answer important questions about chronology, social change, technological levels, relationships among prehistoric peoples and towns, and many other subjects. As evidence, they have the regional variation of prehistoric ceramics, a matter not only of painted designs, but also of clay sources, temper, construction methods, surface treatment, firing techniques, vessel forms, and other characteristics. This ancient pottery yields important information about the prehistoric past. In the same way, the beautiful vessels of the past four hundred years are also subtle statements, reminders of events in the complex world of the pueblos after the coming of Europeans.

Today, most of the Pueblo villages use the same basic technology of pottery-making. Clay is dug, often in dry lumps, out of traditional clay sources known to each village. It is then soaked and cleaned in ways that vary little from town to town. Pots are coil-built, with occasional use of slab-and-pinch techniques; then, the surfaces are finely finished by scraping, wiping, and polishing. Finally, designs are added in slips, natural paints, and manipulations of the clay itself. A few potters use commercial paints, but most traditionalists (potters and collectors) disparage them and opt for pigments made from local plant and mineral sources. A majority of potters prefer the traditional method of dung-firing in outdoor kilns constructed around the pots, though the electric kiln is known and used by some potters because of its greater predictability and the larger number of pots that survive kiln-firing. The higher temperatures of the electric kilns produce harder pottery, which then may be thinner walled than dung-fired pieces.

Despite the basic technological similarities, the great variety of contruction, decoration, and firing techniques available to the modern potter means that a work in clay may take anytime from a few days to many months to complete.

Zuni pot with rosette design, circa 1875, from MNA collections

POTTERS INCLUDED IN "TRADITION AND INNOVATION"

Arroh-ah-och
Angela Baca
Evelyn Cheromiah
Marie Z. Chino
Helen Cordero
Marie Edna Coriz
Popovi Da
Tony Da
Jody Folwell
Laura Gachupin
Rosa Gonzales
Lela Gutierrez
Virginia Gutierrez
Daisy Hooee
Lucy Jojola
Jennie Laate
Lucy M. Lewis
Lenora Lucero
Julian Martinez
Maria Martinez
Ramita Martinez
Eudora Montoya
Tomasita Montoya
Nampeyo
Randy Nahohai
Maria I. Naranjo
Nora Naranjo-Morse
Anacita J. Paca
Carol Pecos
Nicolasa Pena
Anderson Peynetsa
Aurelia Peynetsa
Priscilla Peynetsa
Polly Rose
Ethel Shields
Legoria Tafoya
Manuel Tafoya
Margaret Tafoya
Sarafina Tafoya
Severa Tafoya
Juanita Toledo
Dorothy Trujillo
Tsayutitsa
Cecilia Valencia
Evelyn Vigil
G. Vigil
Lonnie Vigil
Darrell Westika

MAP OF NEW MEXICO'S PUEBLOS

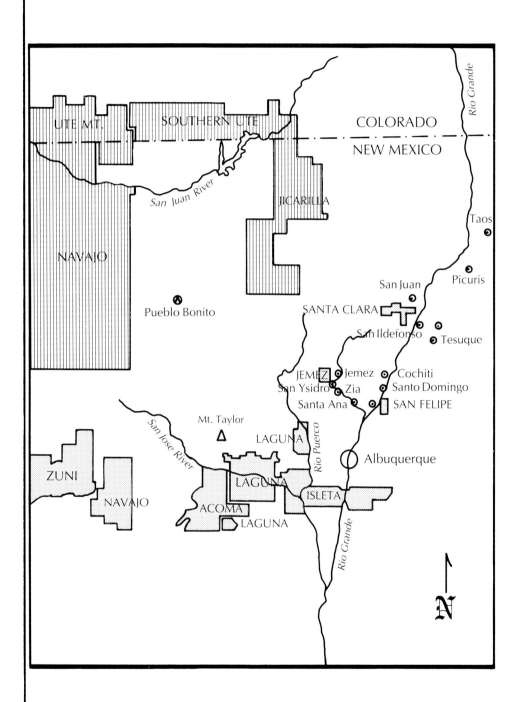

TEWA

Above: San Ildefonso black/red on white pot, circa 1920-1930 (left); San Ildefonso pot, Popovi Da, 1965 (top); San Juan incised polished redware by Tomasita Montoya and San Juan plain polished redware, 1938 (bottom), from MNA collections
Opposite page: Contemporary Santa Clara clay sculpture "Indian girls are not easy!" by Nora Naranjo-Morse, 1989, from MNA collections

*O*f the linguistic groups, the Tewa-speakers are almost certainly the best known potters, primarily through the world-famous pottery of San Ildefonso and Santa Clara. The communities of San Juan, Tesuque, Nambe, and Pojoaque also have had productive ceramic traditions in the twentieth century.

SAN ILDEFONSO

In 1919, a young San Ildefonso man, Julian Martinez, developed a technique of painting black matte slip designs onto the glossy black pottery made by his wife, Maria. He also may have developed a technique of using powdered dung to fire the traditional red San Ildefonso pottery to black in a reducing atmosphere. Most authorities believe

that this was a conscious effort on his part to copy prehistoric pottery from the area. Regardless of whether or not he developed this firing technique, his innovation of the black slip matte painted designs was unquestionably a watershed achievement in the history of Pueblo pottery. It became the trademark of the pottery made by his wife, the woman who preferred to sign her work simply "Maria" but who probably became the most famous Pueblo Indian artist of all time. Working first with Julian and later with other relatives, Maria produced greatly sought-after objects of skill and beauty in a career that spanned nearly eighty years. Her major achievement, however, was not the pottery itself: Maria Martinez's work played a major role in opening a market in the larger world for Pueblo Indian pottery, making it economically feasible for its makers to continue this art form in the twentieth century.

Maria learned to create pottery from her aunt, Nicolasa Pena, making the San Ildefonso Polychrome style typical of the period—black and red designs on a white- or cream-colored background. A red slip line on the rim was common until the end of the nineteenth century when a few potters replaced it with black paint. Pottery expert Jonathan Batkin argues that some potters also occasionally added other details in bright paints after firing. Jars with a sharp demarcation between the body and the flared neck were the most common products of this decorative style, which flourished between 1880 and 1910 in response to a growing tourist market. Late in that period, birds and animals were depicted frequently on the pots. Another common and longer-lived San Ildefonso type had black designs painted on a red body and was made from as early as 1850 until about 1930.

Maria and Julian continued to make the earlier polychrome type until about 1926, while they were refining the black-on-black style. Opportunities to market this style were developing at that time, and the mid-1920s saw a shift at San Ildefonso to a cash economy based primarily on arts and crafts.

The potter Rose Gonzales, who was born at San Juan but married into San Ildefonso and learned pottery there, began working about 1929. She is credited with developing a carved blackware style at the pueblo that also became very popular. With the increasing interest in the blackwares in the late 1920s and early 1930s, the village became an important center in the revival of American Indian arts—and Pueblo pottery in particular. During the height of the Depression, in 1936, unemployment at San Ildefonso was enviably low, and nearly half

of all the employed adults were potters. The women normally built the pots, and the men decorated them with designs like the water serpent (or *avanyu*), feathers, simple geometrical patterns, and life forms. These decorative elements were used on both the black-on-black matte and carved wares and on their red counterparts. They remain characteristic of the types today. Polished plainwares in red and black also have been part of the repertoire throughout.

Maria Martinez worked primarily with her husband until his death in 1944. She usually formed the pots and left the painting to Julian. There are some indications, however, that in times of great demand the Martinezes may have bought greenware pots from other makers and finished them for sale. Other members of the family, including Maria's sisters as well as her sons and daughters-in-law, began making the black-on-black pottery, and the style soon spread to other San Ildefonso potters.

In addition to the black-on-black pots for which she became most famous, Maria Martinez also occasionally made polychrome, polished red, and red-on-red pieces. The few polychrome pieces

San Ildefonso polished blackware vase by Maria Martinez, circa 1930-1940, from MNA collections

made by Maria (and Julian before his death) appear to be mostly unsigned. Maria continued working through 1972; she died in 1980.

In 1956 or 1957, Popovi Da, Maria's son, was responsible for reviving the polychrome style that had largely fallen into disuse with the popularity of the blackwares. He also developed a method for making a black and red two-toned type, though it remained for his son Tony to make it a major focus of work. Recent potters have developed a variety of contemporary styles derived from the San Ildefonso tradition. These include figurines of turtles and bears, turquoise set into pottery, sgraffito decoration, and lidded pottery. They also continue the carved red and black wares for which the village is famous.

In recent years, some potters have revived the polychromes in cream slips on polished redware or on cream or buff backgrounds. The pueblo's figurative pottery tradition also has undergone a revival. As in other villages, Nativity scenes and Storyteller figures have become popular in recent years.

SANTA CLARA

Probably the most prolific of the Pueblo groups in terms of pottery is the village of Santa Clara. The polished red and polished black wares that were the object of experimentation at San Ildefonso were refinements of types that had been common at Santa Clara at least as far back as 1879, when collections were made there for the Smithsonian Institution. A third type, a glistening micaceous ware, also was collected there at the time but appears to have died out as a style shortly after that collection was made. Only a few pieces were produced in the twentieth century. There are also descriptions of a white- or cream-colored slipped type with polychrome decorations, which was no longer made by the beginning of this century, as well as a red-on-tan type. About the same time that this collection was made, a railroad line built across Santa Clara lands brought tourists into the village and with it a market for small, portable versions of these decorative types. A system of water wells further undermined the need for large utilitarian jars, and Santa Clara pottery made the economic transition from household items to works of art in the late nineteenth and early twentieth century. In fact, many water jar forms made after 1930 would be damaged by putting water in them.

A decorative vessel shape commonly associated with Santa Clara is the wedding vase, a jar

Above: Santa Clara redware wedding vase by
Margaret Tafoya (left); Santa Clara blackware
melon bowl by Severa Tafoya (top); Santa Clara
bowl by Lela Gutierrez, 1940 (right); Santa Clara
blackware "bear paw" wedding vase, early 20th
century (bottom); from MNA collections
Right: Contemporary Santa Clara pottery by Polly
Rose (ornate - top and right) and by Jody Folwell
of the Naranjo pottery-making family, 1990
(bottom -plain)
Below: Contemporary Santa Clara melon bowl
by Angela Baca, 1990

form with two spouts. Although we do not know for certain the purpose of the vase, it may be used in a traditional Pueblo wedding ceremony that precedes the Roman Catholic marriage rite. Some authorities have questioned the antiquity of the wedding vase because none of the other Tewa groups had this vessel form or practice. One suggestion is that the type and story were started by a turn-of-the-century Santa Fe trader. Since the Smithsonian Institution has examples of this type collected in 1879, however, there is a problem with this interpretation. Other types common by 1920 were bird effigies, handled cups and vases, stirrup spouts, and "two-storied," waisted water jars.

Potters at Santa Clara imported the black-on-black technology from San Ildefonso in 1927 but were already using other decorative elements—including fluted or scalloped jar-rims, "rainbow bands," and a "bear paw" motif pressed into the body of the still-soft vessel. The last design element is a special emblem of Santa Clara pottery. It is placed on pottery to honor the bear, whom traditional Santa Claras credit with leading the village to water during a life-threatening drought. Pottery experts have traced the motif to sometime in the latter half of the nineteenth century, but the Santa Claras say the drought occurred about four hundred years ago.

An integral part of water jars made during the 1930s and 1940s is the "rainbow band," a raised portion that encircles the jar where the bowl joins the neck. Each of the one, two, or three bands is a prayer to keep the jar's precious contents from evaporating. "Rain drops," small indentations around the top of a jar's rim, likewise are the potter's prayer to keep the water fresh and sweet, according to Mary Ellen and Laurence Blair, biographers of the famous Santa Clara potter Margaret Tafoya.

Carved designs first appeared in the 1920s and may have developed from a series of vessels made in 1922 or 1923 by Sarafina Tafoya. The pots featured bands of deeply impressed animal figures at the pots' shoulders, and these indented designs and fine redware polychromes remained Sarafina's primary styles throughout her life. She was the first of six generations of well-known Tafoya potters at the pueblo. It was Sarafina's children, and in particular her daughter, Margaret Tafoya, who popularized the carved style. These carved designs were especially popular in the 1940s. Common on both the carved and impressed wares is the *avanyu*, or plumed serpent, the guardian of springs,

lakes, and rivers. This motif also is found on pottery from the ancestral Santa Clara site of Puye, occupied from the late thirteenth through the mid-sixteenth centuries.

Potters began to decorate polished red pottery about 1930 with both carving and painting. It was a two-stage process with carved areas being painted in either light red or buff. Realistic scenes and figures have been painted on redwares since about 1940.

Redware vessels were decorated in polychromes as well. These red polychromes, along with the buff types, have persisted to the present. Polychromes are usually red, white, buff, and gray—with painted areas outlined in white clay.

In the 1920 to 1970 revival era, potters developed white and buff polychromes. Two variants of the blackwares included carved surfaces and buff designs painted on the black pottery.

In the 1960s, potters developed a sgraffito technique involving buff areas on polished black and polished redwares. This style has persisted to the present and is often produced in miniature as well. Some of these pots are no larger than 3/8 inch. The market for these finely detailed miniatures has grown substantially in the last few years.

Another interesting phenomenon has been the development of clay figures. Although small figures in clay go back much further in time at Santa Clara (at least to the 1879 Smithsonian collection), they achieved great popularity about 1930. Both Manuel Tafoya, brother of Margaret Tafoya, and Legoria Tafoya created *animalitos* in polished blackware at that time, a type that remains popular.

Santa Clara potters also have developed Storyteller and Nativity scenes out of this figurative tradition. Maria I. Naranjo made Nativities and Storytellers in the mid-to-late 1960s in polished blackware and later in polychrome as well. Other artists also have made these larger figure-types in polished redware. The Santa Clara *animalito* figures appear to have crossed with the Storyteller forms to create two interesting types, Storyteller animals and miniature Storytellers. The Gutierrez family have been innovators across this whole figurative range at Santa Clara.

Another innovator in figurative work is Nora Naranjo-Morse, of the famous Naranjo family of Santa Clara potters. Naranjo-Morse's figures may be as much as five feet high and are often works of great humor as well as beauty. Although she works primarily in clay, Naranjo-Morse creates also in bronze, mixed media, painting, and verse.

SAN JUAN

The polished redware that is a secondary color at San Ildefonso and Santa Clara is the primary type at the Pueblo of San Juan. Although it is possible to find the blackware at San Juan, it is the less common form. Traditionally, potters polished only on the upper portion of the redware and left the vessels undecorated or decorated only by small lumps of clay. This style dates to the seventeenth century Spanish period. A red-on-tan ware also was common at San Juan in the nineteenth century. We have one example of a black and red-on-white polychrome vessel that dates to the late nineteenth century. Pottery-making nearly died out at San Juan prior to the revival of the art about 1930.

After 1930, potters inspired by archaeological finds from excavations near their village began to use other forms of decoration. Many of these design elements continue to be popular. Potters use sharp tools to make bands of incised decoration, and these unslipped bands show the glittery flecks characteristic of the micaceous clays of the area.

Most of the decorations are geometrical forms, cross-hatching and chevrons, though floral and figural motifs do occur in recent examples. Potters sometimes paint matte colors between the incised lines or fill in the shapes created by those lines. Tomasita Montoya, whose incised work is illustrated here, is considered by many to be the most influential potter working at San Juan.

Carved forms also occur at San Juan, sometimes combined with incising, sometimes alone in forms difficult to distinguish from those of Santa Clara and San Ildefonso. Some potters now make polychromes as well, a few in muted matte colors of sand, tan, red, white, and gray and others in bright commercial paints.

A few San Juan potters have made Storyteller figures. In general, however, the recent revival of Pueblo ceramic sculpture has not played a major part in San Juan contemporary ceramics.

TESUQUE

Traditional Tesuque polychrome pottery, now quite rare, had very elaborate black floral designs

Tesuque rain god figurines (left) and Tesuque pitcher with black floral on cream, red base, early 1900s (right); from MNA collections

11

in distinct bands on a cream background. These pots, common between 1830 and 1910, also had a red base that constituted approximately the bottom third of the vessel. Potters also made a black-on-red type for a short time around the turn of the century.

The commercial sale of the pottery, primarily in smaller and simplified forms, was economically important in the village in the early years of the twentieth century but declined after about 1935. Pottery made for sale to tourists from the 1890s into the 1930s occasionally was painted with blue and purple and other unusual colors after firing. Although the earlier pieces are relatively subtle in tones, bright, sometimes garish poster paints replaced the earlier pigments by the 1920s.

Today, only a few traditionally styled Tesuque pots are being made. However, a textured red-on-tan type that harks back to red-on-tan vessels of the nineteenth and early twentieth centuries is growing in popularity.

Tesuque's best-known ceramics are a series of controversial "Rain God" figurines made in large quantities in the late nineteenth and early twentieth centuries. Often painted in bright colors, these small figurines were sold all over the United States in boxes of Gunther Candy between 1900 and 1940.

Although often disparaged by scholars and museum curators as tawdry curios made at the direction of a trader, at least one expert on Pueblo figurative pottery, Barbara Babcock, has argued convincingly that they were direct outgrowths of a long Pueblo tradition. We do know that Tesuque small, seated figurines were collected by early ethnologists James and Matilda Coxe Stevenson for the Smithsonian Institution as early as 1878 in a plain micaceous type, a blackware, and a buff-slipped type with painted red and black designs.

After 1900, potters added a white-slipped type with red and blue designs, then replaced it in the 1920s with a tan clay decorated with bright poster paints. More recently, larger Storyteller types and pottery scenes of Pueblo life, Nativities, and Storytellers have gained acceptance with a few Tesuque potters.

NAMBE

A polished blackware similar to that made traditionally at Santa Clara supplanted polychromes at Nambe Pueblo about 1825. This blackware was softer in paste than the Santa Clara version and had a slight sheen caused by the micaceous clays of Nambe. Potters continued to make a few of these vessels at Nambe until about 1950. They also made natural-colored micaceous and mica-slipped pots of the general type more often associated with Taos and Picuris.

After a serious decline, pottery has undergone a recent revival at Nambe and its close neighbor, Pojoaque. Today's styles include a textured matte polychrome pottery, a polished background polychrome, and some polished red and black wares, and various figurative types—including Storytellers.

Contemporary Nambe jar made with micaceous clay by Lonnie Vigil, 1990

POJOAQUE

Pojoaque has participated in the same pottery revival as Nambe, and the two villages' ceramic histories have been quite similar. Both villages were making polychrome types in the eighteenth century. Pojoaque also produced a version of polished blackware, somewhat harder and less micaceous than Nambe's, in the nineteenth century.

Today, most Pojoaque potters make the polished red and black wares and polychromes also made at Nambe. Current styles also include polychromes featuring pastel colors on tan, buff, cream, or polished red backgrounds. Occasionally, a few potters also make jars similar to the old eighteenth-century polychrome style and a few small animal forms.

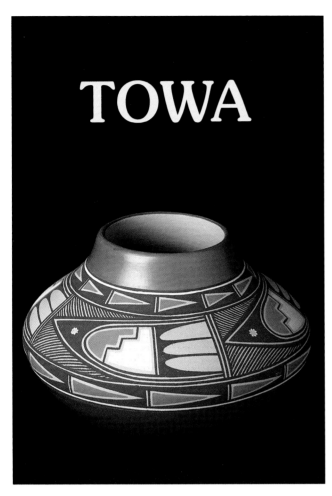

TOWA

Above: Jemez polychrome on buff jar by Laura Gachupin, 1979, from MNA collections
Below: Contemporary Jemez seed pot by G. Vigil and wedding vase by Carol Pecos, 1990

Jemez Tesuque poster paint pot, 1967-1969, from MNA collections

JEMEZ

*P*rior to the Pueblo Revolt of 1680, the Towa-speaking pueblo of Jemez made a carbon paint, fine-line black-on-white ware, interesting for being the only pottery of that type fired in a reducing atmosphere. The making of ceramic vessels all but ceased in the village in the period between 1680 and the 1940s. During these years, almost all of the pottery made in Jemez was produced by women who had married into the

13

village. In the years in which little or no pottery was made at the pueblo, the Jemez traded for pottery from Zia.

In the 1940s, a Zia woman came to Jemez as a bride. Her family members were the first of the new Jemez potters, and other Jemez women quickly learned the art as well. At first, the new pottery was painted with bright show-card colors, but with the beginning of the Indian arts revival of the 1950s, a style similar to traditional San Juan redwares developed.

By the 1980s, only a few potters were using the poster paints, but the use of orange, white, and black acrylic paints on tan paste vessels was increasing. Another type of pottery found at Jemez has brown paint on a tan slip—sometimes with terra cotta and black elements as well. This Jemez type can be identified by its distinctive black designs and occasional turquoise elements. A few pieces also have been painted with natural earth pigments. One family, the Gachupins, also has developed a style using natural orange and black painted corn and geometrical designs on a buff background. Most firing at Jemez is done in electric kilns.

Despite the small number of pottery vessels produced at Jemez in the first half of this century, potters were making figurines and *animalitos*, and this figural tradition has expanded in recent years. Jemez is one of the most prolific pueblos in the creation of Storytellers and other clay scenes such as Nativities. Storyteller expert Barbara Babcock states that there were more than 60 potters making figures there in the mid-1980s. The Jemez versions are a tan slip with dark brown and sometimes red-brown and black lines.

Another interesting recent phenomenon at Jemez is the re-creation of a fifteenth to sixteenth century glazeware once made at Pecos Pueblo. Pecos, also a Towa-speaking village, was abandoned in 1838 when its last seventeen inhabitants moved to Jemez, where their descendants still live and retain their Pecos identity. Two of these descendants, Juanita Toledo and Evelyn Vigil, recreated the type, which is a redware with dark brown glaze paint outlining cream design elements. There is a "spirit break" in the rim-line. Other modern Pecos pots are black and orange designs on a light orange body.

Today, Jemez has a robust pottery industry. Ties to Zia remain close, however, and ceremonial vessels made at Zia often are used in Jemez ceremonies.

TIWA

*T*he Tiwa-speaking pueblos include Taos, Picuris, Isleta, Sandia, and the Texas pueblo Ysleta del Sur. Little remains of a continuous ceramic tradition in any of these pueblos, though Taos and Picuris have continued some production of a type of pottery introduced early in the period of Spanish and Native American contact.

TAOS

Historic period pottery from Taos and its neighboring northern pueblos, including Picuris, was a black-on-white carbon paint ware until the Pueblo

14

Taos bean pot, 1700s (left) and Picuris micaceous bean pot by Ramita Martinez, 1959 (right), from MNA collections

Revolt of 1680. At the time of the revolt, the micaceous type now usually associated with those pueblos largely replaced this decorated ware. Potters use a glittering light brown or golden clay to produce ceramics similar to those of the nearby Jicarilla Apache. Fire-cloudings are common on the shiny surfaces of pots, and punched and applique elements are the only forms of decoration.

Over the years, potters have produced a number of interesting vessel shapes. Since the focus is clearly on considerations of utility, the makers often add handles and lids to enhance that useful-

ness. This tendency toward utility is demonstrated clearly by Taos' best-known form—the bean pot.

Historically, only a few figurines have been made at Taos. Most of the potters from Taos who have participated in the figurative pottery revival have been Jemez women who married into the pueblo.

PICURIS

The ceramic history of Picuris is similar to that of Taos, having its roots in the northern Rio Grande black-on-white wares and then, after 1680, turning primarily to the micaceous pottery heavily influenced by Athabaskan prototypes. Picuris vessels are hard-fired, thin-walled, and lighter in color than those of Taos. Potters use the same golden or brown clay to produce a few human and animal figures.

ISLETA

The earliest known pottery from Isleta was a plain red-brown ware, but from about the turn of the century to the 1940s, a polychrome type of black, white, and red designs replaced it. This change occurred either because Isleta potters were heavily influenced by Laguna potters of that period or because the pottery was being made by Laguna refugees. Many of these pieces are small bowls, sometimes with twisted handles, that are painted with simple designs.

Recently, there has been some revival of this early polychrome by Laguna descendants living at Isleta. These pots have a light red base and a black and red-on-white geometrical design band on the upper part of the pot. Occasionally, pottery makers glaze the interiors of their pieces.

Since 1950, nontraditional methods have characterized Isleta pottery. Poster paints decorated pottery in the 1950s. Today, a commercial white slip pottery with decorations in orange and dark brown is most popular. Some Isleta potters work in both traditional forms and the figurative Storytellers and Nativities popular in other villages.

SANDIA AND YSLETA DEL SUR

These two pueblos have produced very little pottery in the twentieth century. Both had a few producing potters into the 1930s, but pottery making virtually ceased after that. In the past twenty years, there have been a small number of red-and-black on cream vessels produced at both pueblos in an attempt to revive the art. Ysleta del Sur pottery often says "Tiguex" on the base.

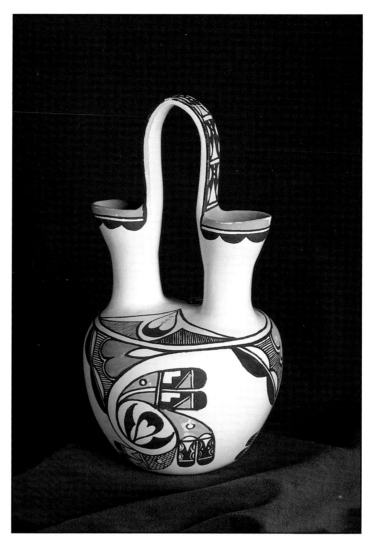

Right: Isleta wedding vase, black/red poly-chrome on white by Lucy Jojola, 1972, from MNA collections

Below: Prehistoric Puebloan pottery (clockwise from left: Mimbres black-on-white bowl, circa AD 1100-1350; Reserve black-on-white pitcher, circa AD 925-1275; Pinedale black-on-white pitcher, circa AD 1275-1325; Linofugitive red jar, circa AD 575-775; Tusayan polychrome ladle, circa 1150-1300) from MNA collections

Opposite page: Zuni pot, probably early 20th century, from MNA collections

KERES

Cochiti storyteller by Helen Cordero,
1965, from MNA collections

*T*he pottery of the Keres-speaking pueblos—
Acoma, Zia, Santo Domingo, Cochiti, San
Felipe, Laguna, and Santa Ana—usually features
elaborate black or black-and-red natural and geometrical motifs on a white or cream background.
Pottery has remained an active tradition at most of
these conservative pueblos, with the exception of
Laguna and Santa Ana, where the art nearly died
out in the 1940s, and San Felipe, which has had
little ceramic production since about 1700.

ZIA

Since the Pueblo of Zia has poor agricultural
lands, it has long depended on trade as an important source of income. One of these trade goods
was their pottery, a strong, thick-walled, high-
fired ware. An early type identified with Zia also
occurred at Santa Ana. Called Puname Polychrome, it was common from 1700 to 1760 at both
places. Potters decorated a cream-slipped, brick-
red body with black mineral designs (usually
feather symbols and arcs). They also put narrow
bands of red around the lower body of the pot and
the rim.

The shapes of the Puname Polychrome pieces
are quite distinctive. On bowls, there is a sharp
bend below the major design field. The jar form's
greatest width is very low on the vessel—with the
area below sharply undercut.

Zia jars in the next period, up to 1800, were
spherical, with a short, undecorated neck. Rims
were painted red before 1780, black thereafter.
Wide and narrow bands alternate in the main
design field, and there are often red arcs in the
design. In the next fifty years (1800-1850), designs
became bolder and more crudely executed, with
red banding at the bottom. Following this period
of change, the type stabilized into what now is
called Zia Polychrome—a type that remains very
popular today.

Zia Polychrome has bird and floral patterns
and a wavy, sometimes double red line with the
distinctive Zia split-tailed birds both over and
under the line. This thick-walled, well-formed
pottery has mineral paint floral motifs of black
with some red elements. Occasionally, potters use
a pale gold color as well. A distinctive feature of
the pottery is a crushed black basalt temper that is
apparent on the surface of the pot—even through
the decoration. The base clay is gray; the design
background is a cream or gray-white, and the
pottery is extremely hard-fired. Zia Polychrome
jar forms are characterized by high shoulders, and
occasional pots now have a red-slipped base rather
than just a red band around the bottom of the main
design field.

Zia pottery styles also include redware with
black-painted traditional Zia designs. Another
recent development is decorating vessels after they
have been fired with acrylic paintings of various
older designs, such as birds or sun symbols, along
with detailed figures of dancers or other important
Zia images. These pieces usually have black or
white backgrounds.

SANTA ANA

Having grown out of the same eighteenth century Puname Polychrome tradition that produced Zia pottery, Santa Ana pottery is understandably similar to Zia's. It, too, has mineral paints, brick-red clay, and feather and arc designs. Santa Ana work, however, began to diverge from the Zia style about 1820. Wide red bands in the design field often contain unpainted crescent areas within them, showing the cream-colored slip beneath. Another difference is the frequent absence of black edging at the contact between red- and cream-painted areas.

The surface of Santa Ana pottery was a rich tan until 1880, but vessels after that were more nearly white. At the same time, the design work became sloppier. This style was popular until about 1920, but by the 1940s Santa Ana potters had almost ceased production on this and virtually every other type of pottery.

One potter, Eudora Montoya, is credited with preserving the style virtually alone for some forty years until a revival began in the 1970s. Montoya and her students are careful to preserve traditional designs and techniques, using old clay pits, sand temper, natural paints, and outdoor firing. Old designs now back in use include turkey eyes, clouds, lightning, rainbows, and crosses. The current version has blocky red designs, broad lines, distorted triangles, and scallops. Design is sparser than in early examples of the type.

COCHITI

The Pueblo of Cochiti has an extremely conservative pottery tradition, its history since 1780 dominated by only two basically simultaneous types. Kiua Polychrome (1780-1920, plus a few more recent examples) is black and red on a gray surface, with the underbody marked by the typical Keres red band. Designs are bold geometrics, and as at Zia, the rim top changed from red to black about the end of the eighteenth century. Potters seldom painted bowl interiors, though one occasionally finds an intentional row of dots inside that appear to be made by shaking a paintbrush over that interior surface. The pots have a grit and crushed quartz temper, leading to a slightly gritty surface on the pot. A close look at this surface often reveals striations made by wiping the still-wet surface with a rag in the finishing process.

Cochiti Polychrome (1830 to the present) has a light floral design that often incorporates sacred elements such as semicircular figures representing clouds, parallel lines coming down from another figure (rain), and the zigzag elements that denote lightning. This use of the most overtly sacred symbols directly on pottery is quite unusual in Pueblo pottery. Representations of birds, animals, and humans are also common, along with a virtually invariable line break in the black rimtop. It also has the temper and wiped surface typical of historic Keres pottery.

Today, Cochiti potters make a variety of bowls, jars, and figurines. Pots are simple in design with black-on-gray or creamy white bodies and brick-red bases and interiors. The main design field, though framed by lines from the upper and lower areas of the vessel, is not divided into framed rectangular fields, called "panels," thus contributing to the sense of isolation of these designs. The black lines are fine, and decorative elements often exist in complete isolation from other figures on the same pot. Red elements are used in the designs only occasionally.

Cochiti was one of the pueblos that produced the controversial "Rain God" figurines in the late nineteenth and early twentieth centuries. Another development in the 1930s may have presaged a major 1980s interest in Cochiti ceramic figures. At that time, potters produced a variety of effigy pottery, as well as many small, independent representations of humans and animals. Animal figurines have been common at the pueblo for some two-hundred years. Most of these figures appear on a polychrome of cream, red-brown, and black. Through the first sixty years of the twentieth century, however, the figurines dwindled in size, and themes from pueblo life itself became the primary

Cochiti black/white on gray pot, circa 1918 (left) and bird figurine, circa 1898 (right), from MNA collections

depictions. It was the representation of the Story-teller that renewed the public's interest in Pueblo ceramic figures.

Currently, Cochiti probably is best known as the home of Helen Cordero, whose Storyteller figures inspired this rebirth of interest in Pueblo figurative pottery. Cordero makes a variety of these types—Nativity scenes, singing mothers, drummers, and other characters from Pueblo life. She created her first Storyteller figure in 1964 and has received countless prizes and awards for these pieces in the years since. Her figures usually have their eyes closed and mouths wide open. Other details vary tremendously in hairstyle, designs on clothing, and number and placement of children. Like most Cochiti figures, her creations are modeled in the creamy Cochiti clay with black and red-brown details.

In the 1980s, Barbara Babcock noted fifty-five potters making Storytellers at Cochiti. Many of them were working also in "Animal Storytellers," an apparent combination of the Storyteller and *animalito* ideas. These animal figures frequently have Cochiti pottery designs painted on them. Recently, two male potters from Hopi who live at Cochiti have made Storyteller versions involving Pueblo sacred clowns called Mudheads. For religious reasons, Cochiti-born potters do not depict these sacred figures for sale.

SAN FELIPE

San Felipe Pueblo appears to have lost most of its ceramic tradition by 1700. Although potters continued to make utility vessels, they produced little in the way of decorated wares after that time. Today, there are only a few potters in the village, and their vessels are heavy and crudely decorated. The basic designs are much simplified versions of those being made at Cochiti and Santo Domingo— black designs on a grayish slip or a few pieces with red decoration on a tan base. Fire-clouding is quite common.

Two potters currently living at San Felipe participated in the figurative pottery upsurge in the 1970s and 1980s. However, neither is a San Felipe native. Leonora Lucero is one of the Loretto sisters of the well-known Jemez pottery-making family, while the other, Cecilia Valencia, is the daughter of another Loretto sister, Dorothy Trujillo. Both potters use Jemez clays and colors.

Zia bird/floral polychrome on gold background, circa 1898 (left) and canteen, circa 1900 (right), from MNA collections

20

Santo Domingo commercial glaze jar by Anacita J. Paca, 1972 (left) and black/cream on buff, circa 1898 (right), from MNA collections

SANTO DOMINGO

The current style, Santo Domingo Polychrome, developed from the same Kiua Polychrome style as the Cochiti types. Paneling of the main design field makes Santo Domingo versions easy to recognize, for this practice is not followed at Cochiti.

Between 1880 and 1920, the most typical pots had black-on-cream or buff rows or arrangements of repeated, similar, black geometrical forms. From about 1900 to the present, jars were taller than the Kiua forms, with a flaring rim. Birds and flowers were common designs, though often enclosed by the earlier geometrical forms. Only occasionally are red elements used in the main design fields of Santa Domingo vessels, though this practice seems to be increasing. After about 1925, there was an all-over red slip below the design area, rather than merely a red band. The black lines on the rims of Santo Domingo pottery also have a conspicuous spirit break.

Early in the twentieth century, potters produced small pots, often with handles, for the tourist market. Many of these followed traditional Santo Domingo design canons and technology, though a few were among the poster-paint types produced by various pueblos. Recently, a few potters have painted tourist wares with bright housepaints, while others are using commercial glazes. It is characteristic of this pueblo (which is highly conservative yet has a long history of outside trade) that it simultaneously makes extremely traditional Santo Domingo wares for use in the village and a series of very nontraditional pieces aimed exclusively at the tourist market.

Traditional religious beliefs prevent making figurative pottery for sale at Santo Domingo, as is true also at San Felipe, Santa Ana, and Zia. Only Marie Edna Coriz, another of the Loretto sisters from Jemez, makes Storyteller figures.

Contemporary Acoma turtle canteen and corn canteen by Ethel Shields, 1990

ACOMA

Contemporary Acoma pottery has developed from a series of whitewares with black and red mineral matte paint. Historically, potters used sherd-tempered, dark gray clay, which they slipped white and decorated with a red rim. From 1700 to 1760, designs were delicate and carefully executed on short-necked jars; 1760 to 1830 saw a lengthened neck, bolder designs, and often a volute of red around the body of the vessel, which potters edged in black matte paint. The rim was painted black in this later period, as in other Keresan pueblos, and the base clay was sometimes brown or tan. From the late nineteenth century to the present, potters have added red-orange and black geometrical and bird designs to the slip of the traditional polychromes.

Small bird figures and effigy vessels were made in the late nineteenth century at Acoma, and figurines also are known from the 1940s. Acoma pottery designs remained the least changed of any pueblo in the first half of the twentieth century. Important innovations, however, have been made in the last few decades.

Today, pottery makers frequently decorate their pieces with a fine-line, black hachured design called *samumu* and with human and animal motifs borrowed from the ancient pottery of the Mimbres, a prehistoric group that once lived to the south of Acoma's territory. These designs were introduced and suggested by Dr. Kenneth Chapman of the Museum of New Mexico to Lucy M. Lewis, matriarch of one of the two major families of Acoma potters. In addition, Lucy Lewis borrowed the Zuni heart-line deer motif and made it a common contemporary design in Acoma pottery. Another group of important Acoma potters, the family of the late Marie Z. Chino, also uses these designs.

It is from the 1930s on that the use of geometrical and/or floral patterns to fill the design field fairly uniformly gave way to extensive white spaces with only one or a few versions of a single motif, such as the heart-line deer, scattered on them. In the post-war period, potters began borrowing motifs from the Tularosa Black-on-White prehistoric ware for their pieces. Corrugated whiteware vessels and a few white-on-black types round out the types of pottery found today.

Today's Acoma pottery is of excellent quality—thin-walled, hard-fired, and carefully painted.

Geometrical designs often are black-on-white, and designs from nature usually are executed in a polychrome that brings in red designs as well. Bases are slipped red-orange.

Small bird and animal figurines are common, as well as the larger figurative scenes—Storytellers, Nativities, etc. The bottom halves of these large figures are often traditional Acoma pottery designs and bowl forms, which may or may not have legs sticking out of them. These pieces have the distinctive stark-white kaolin slip background familiar from pottery vessels, with black and red line detailing.

Another style distinctive to Acoma and its neighbor Zuni is the combination of figurative and vessel forms—a small animal crawling on a vessel or figures climbing out of a bowl.

Acoma jar, circa 1940, from MNA collections

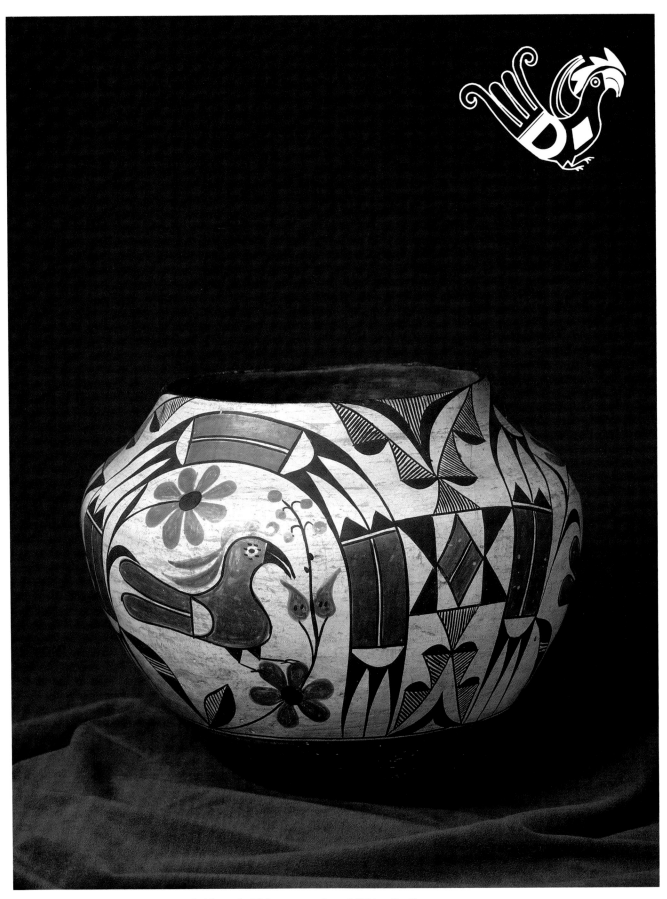

Black/red on white Acoma pot, probably early 20th century, from MNA collections

Laguna polychrome on white (left) and Laguna "copy" of Zuni style, probably by Arroh-ah-och, circa 1910 (right), pottery from MNA collections

LAGUNA

Pottery at Laguna developed from the same early traditions as that of Acoma and is a kaolin-slipped whiteware with black paint and other oxide paints of yellow, red, and brown. Often, there is red paint on the interior of bowls, and strokes of red frequently decorated the inside of the jars. Cross-hatching is common, as are yellow, red, and black solid designs. Patterns use both geometrical and life-form designs that are similar to those from Acoma. Traditionally, however, Laguna pottery was thicker-walled and the designs not as precisely executed. Arroh-ah-och, a male transvestite potter, also produced copies of Zuni designs on Laguna jars from about 1880 to 1900.

Little pottery was produced between the 1940s and the 1970s, when the art underwent a revival. During these years, Evelyn Cheromiah continued the tradition virtually alone until, with the help of her skills, a federal grant, and enthusiastic students, it was possible to recreate the pottery industry at Laguna.

ZUNI

The Pueblo of Zuni is unique in many ways, including its primarily white-slipped ceramic tradition. The pottery bears some remote similarities to the pottery of Acoma, its nearest Pueblo neighbor.

About 1700, Zuni glazeware pottery was replaced by mineral matte black paint decorations in two design bands. The midbody decoration was formal and geometrical, the upper body band more elaborate and floral. The base was red, as was the line, or *onanne*, around the rim. A rare, crudely painted white-on-red ware also existed briefly in the late nineteenth century.

Potters usually decorated historic Zuni pottery with stylized plant, bird, and deer motifs as well as repeated geometrical units in black, red, and a range of browns on a white-slipped background. In the early nineteenth century, geometrics included a spiral form derived from the "rain bird," as well as asymmetrical rectilinear designs filled in with diagonal cross-hatching. By late in the century, the geometrics were less common and the life forms (plant and animal) more characteristic. The deer with a red heart-line, dating to

Zuni rainbird design by Tsayutitsa, 1920s (left) and heart-line deer, late 19th century (right), from MNA collections

26

Above: Zuni fetish bowls, late 19th or early 20th century, featuring animal motifs and stepped sides, from MNA collections
Right: Zuni owls (top, right 1935; lower, right 1961), from MNA collections

approximately 1860 as a motif, is a particularly distinctive Zuni trait, as is a small bird form normally used as a small filler element in Zuni design. This motif is thought to date to approximately 1835. A large medallion, or rosette, also became common on vessels of the late nineteenth century—as did feather representations, which remain popular.

In addition to the plant and animal designs used on food and water vessels, there are animal designs and appliques used only on vessels associated with religious traditions. These seem to remain constant through the nineteenth and twentieth century. These include water-associated animals (such as tadpoles, frogs, and dragonflies) as well as butterflies. These designs are found on the step-sided bowls which the Zuni call "fetish bowls." Often, the Zuni use these vessels to hold cornmeal.

Figurative forms, including birds, game animals, and domestic creatures, also were common long into the prehistoric past. At Zuni, ducks and owls were particularly common in the last two centuries, but only the owl became well known to collectors. Because of its popularity, potters here continued to make it into the twentieth century, often with small owls perched on its wings or back.

These owlets have caused the figurines to be confused with the Storyteller animals made in some other pueblos, but the Zuni potters deny the connection, saying that they are simply owls with their children. The form long precedes the current enthusiasm for Storytellers. Duck effigies also have made a comeback in the 1980s, including several by Anderson and Priscilla Peynetsa at the Museum of Northern Arizona's 1988 Zuni Artist Exhibition. The Peynetsas also have experimented in the late 1980s with modeling the *Kolowisi* (the feathered serpent) on pottery, a figure seen on some late nineteenth century bowls. In 1989 to 1990 lizard effigies appeared as well.

Combinations of the various types of motifs from historic pottery are common in Zuni vessels today, but the colors have been changed to red and brownish-black on white or buff backgrounds, a more limited palette than the earlier versions. A black-on-red ware also is becoming common. As anthropologist Margaret Hardin has noted, the historic period at Zuni is replete with examples and reports of copying designs from older pots, usually with some modification. At Zuni, these periodic revivals of old styles appear to be an indigenous phenomenon, rather than one suggested by an anthropologist, trader, or archaeological investigation.

Development and change in pottery at Zuni are unlike those of other pueblos in that they are responses to internal pottery use in the village, rather than to a commercial market. Although some Zuni pottery has been sold outside of Zuni, much more of it has been kept for family use or to be given as gifts.

Accordingly, pottery-making at Zuni decreased thoughout most of the twentieth century. In the 1980s, however, it is in a cycle of revival again. A potter from Acoma, Jennie Laate, married into Zuni and has taught the art to many high school students; Daisy Hooee, granddaughter of the Hopi potter Nampeyo, also has conducted classes of various types. The forms made by these women and their students, however, are uniquely Zuni and derived primarily from studying historic Zuni ceramics. Both dung-fired and kiln-fired pottery are now common at Zuni.

Zuni pot, probably early 20th century, from MNA collections

The extreme popularity of Zuni pottery in MNA's annual Zuni Artist Exhibition, which began in 1987, has opened another large market for the pottery, and show entries in that category have increased greatly each year. The 1987-90 period has seen burgeoning in both numbers and innovation in the pottery entered in the show.

Above: Contemporary Zuni duck effigy pot by Anderson and Aurelia Peynetsa, 1988
Opposite page: Contemporary Zuni pots by Anderson and Aurelia Peynetsa, 1990 (right pot in MNA collections)

CONCLUSION

*P*ottery making remains a vital living tradition in virtually all of the New Mexico pueblos, preserved as a matter of both economy and tradition. As it passed out of use as a day-to-day household object, the pottery grew instead at most pueblos into a way of participating in the larger cash economy of the United States. At the same time, it continued to fulfill important social and ritual needs within the community, needs often linked closely to village identity and pride. In a few pueblos, these two functions were split between two separate types of pottery. The low prices commanded by Indian pottery early in this century caused a further splitting, the development of a curio-type produced only for tourists and a finer ware for more traditional uses.

With periodic renewed interest by collectors, beginning in the 1930s and occurring most recently from the 1970s to the present, a market has developed for high-quality pottery as fine art, with the result that the same excellent work can fulfill both economic and traditional functions. The number of fine pieces, both traditional forms and the innovative styles developing out of them, has risen sharply as a result, while curio-types have declined in numbers and importance. With this resurgence, the pottery of the New Mexico pueblos remains a varied and vital arena for artists and collectors alike. These works of great skill and beauty have found their audience in lovers of Native American art and assured themselves a future to match their long and honored past.

ABOUT THE AUTHOR

Dr. Linda B. Eaton is Curator of Ethnology at the Museum of Northern Arizona and coordinator of the Museum's annual Zuni, Hopi, and Navajo Artist Exhibitions. A graduate of Rice University in anthropology and fine arts/art history, she received her M.A. and Ph.D. in anthropology from Brown University. Much of her work is concerned with art in society, and she has followed this interest through the Middle East, Africa, the realm of the Maya, and, most of all, in Zuni and other parts of the southwestern United States.

SUGGESTED READING

Babcock, Barbara A. and Guy and Doris Monthan
1986 *The Pueblo Storyteller.* University of Arizona Press, Tucson.

Batkin, Jonathan
1987 *Pottery of the Pueblos of New Mexico 1700-1940.* Taylor Museum of the Colorado Springs Fine Arts Center, Colorado Springs.

Blair, Mary Ellen and Laurence
1986 *Margaret Tafoya: A Tewa Potter's Heritage and Legacy.* Schiffer, West Chester, Pa.

Bunzel, Ruth L.
1972 *The Pueblo Potter.* Dover, New York.

Dedera, Don
1985 *Artistry in Clay.* Northland Press, Flagstaff.

Hardin, Margaret A.
1983 *Gifts of Mother Earth: Ceramics in the Zuni Tradition.* Heard Museum, Phoenix.

Harlow, Francis H.
1970 *Historic Pueblo Indian Pottery.* Museum of New Mexico Press, Santa Fe.

Harlow, Francis H. and John V. Young
1972 *Contemporary Pueblo Indian Pottery.* Museum of New Mexico Press, Santa Fe.

LeFree, Betty
1975 *Santa Clara Pottery Today.* University of New Mexico Press for the School of American Research, Albuquerque.

Maxwell Museum of Anthropology
1974 *Seven Families in Pueblo Pottery.* University of New Mexico Press, Albuquerque.

Peterson, Susan
1984 *Lucy M. Lewis: American Indian Potter.* Kodansha International, Tokyo.

Rodee, Marian and James Ostler
1986 *Zuni Pottery.* Schiffer, West Chester, Pa.

Trimble, Stephen
1987 *Talking with the Clay.* School of American Research, Santa Fe.

All photographs by Gene Balzer

All motifs and borders taken from "North American Indian Designs for Artists and Craftspeople" by Eva Wilson, published by Dover Publications, Inc., New York

Catalog Numbers:
p. 4 - E1943; p. 6 - (clockwise starting left) E7739, E3579, E8959, E399; p. 8 - E7453; p. 9 - top photograph (clockwise starting left) E7708, E7710, E7707, E5248; p. 11 - (left to right) E4454, E4479, E7721; p. 13 - top, left photograph - E8965; right photograph - E7477; p. 14 - E5058 (left); p. 15 - E1898; p. 16 - top photograph - E5903; p. 17 - E7191; p. 18 - E7345; p. 19 - E861(left) and E402 (right); p. 20 - E1240 (left) and E4452 (right); p. 21 - E5747 (left) and E382 (right); p. 23 - E1233; p. 24 - E6735; p. 25 - E6683 (left) and E4011 (right); p. 26 & 27 - E1943 (left) and E6696 (right); p. 28 top photograph - E6699 (left) and E6697 (right); bottom photograph - (clockwise starting left) - E6713, E52, E2364; p. 29 - E7191; p. 31 - right E9481

Plateau Managing Editor: Diana Clark Lubick
Graphic Design by Dianne Moen Zahnle
Color Separations by American Color
Typography by MacTypeNet
Printing by Land O'Sun Printers